Landscape Photography

10 Essential Tips to Take Your Landscape Photography to The Next Level

James Carren

Table of Contents

Introduction

Landscape photography is a difficult craft that looks deceivingly simple. Often, photographers go out to shoot an image, which through their eye and lens looks lush, verdant, pastoral, or otherwise entrancing, and come away wondering why the pictures are flat, devoid of life, or uninteresting.

In this book, I will give you a multitude of techniques and tips for taking landscape photographs and to otherwise improve your skill. It doesn't matter if you've taken landscape photos before or not, I feel confident that something here will help you to think of landscapes in a new way.

One of the most important points of this book—which I will be reiterating constantly—is that you have to get into the habit of *seeing*. Just because you look around you each day, doesn't mean you see. It is a skill that must be learned, but which is learned fluidly, intuitively, and through lots of practice. Seeing includes understanding and noticing things such as light conditions, composition, and the psychology of how colors affect the feel and tone of your image. The fun part is, that once you've learned to really see, you will notice that everyone sees differently. Two different people can take a photo of the same landscape in the same spot at the same time of day, and these images, even before processing, will look completely different.

Aside from this ability which must be honed, you will also learn how to handle your camera better. For most people, this can be the most intimidating part about photography. I'm not going to overwhelm you with complicated equations or explanations. However, it is important that you know the basics of how to control your camera so that you spend less time fixing the photos after you take them. There are also a couple of technical tricks that can help your images stand out.

Landscape photography, like anything else, requires practice. I will discuss a few simple techniques to get you into the habit of taking pictures each day. Finally, I'll talk about post-processing, and how you can use it, in combination with your unique way of seeing, to manipulate what your viewer sees and feels.

Chapter 1
What is a Landscape?

When you Google search the word landscape, here is the definition you get: all the visible features of an area of countryside or land, often considered in terms of their aesthetic appeal.

Very broadly, this also applies to the art of landscape photography itself. In essence, any picture of the land is a landscape. In contemporary photography, however, there are a multitude of different techniques and styles that can qualify as a landscape. The rule of thumb in my mind is, as long as it has a horizon line, it's a landscape. Even with this rule, however, there are a few types of photographs waver between what is considered landscape and what is considered abstract. Things like this might include a detailed shot of a flower or piece of bark, or an image of the sky or sea in which no horizon line can be seen. These kinds of pictures can often be included in portfolios with landscape, because of the unclear border between genres.

That said, let's focus on the more common types of landscape photography. Firstly, let's address landscape format. As most of you know, this is when the image is shot and/or displayed horizontally, which makes sense due to the horizon line. Most landscape photographs do read in this way, but they don't have to.

Landscapes don't all have to be dreamy and pastoral scenes, either. They can be dramatic and focus on the weather, like the stunning photographs taken of violent thunderstorms and tornadoes. They don't have to be devoid of buildings, either; landscapes are there to be taken no matter where you live. Specifically, a landscape with many buildings is known as an urban landscape, or cityscape.

If you're a photographer who typically enjoys taking portraits, and this is a foray into a whole new world for you, try taking images of people in landscapes. With this method, the people aren't the focus, but they can provide a good sense of scale or human presence to the image. If you choose, for example, to make the people in the landscape incredibly miniscule, it can serve to emphasize the grand stature of something natural, be it a giant redwood or a towering wave.

Within the genre of landscape painting, there are three main categories. These apply to landscape photography as well. They are Realism (or Modernism), Impressionism (or Pictorialism), and Abstraction.

Realism is exactly what it sounds like. You take a picture of what's in front of you, and then when you process it, you make it look as much like reality as possible. This would include things like matching the white balance to how it looked outside, and making sure that the color was as close to true as you could get it. Really, I feel that this method of shooting doesn't allow much room for expression beyond choice of composition.

Pictures such as these bring the Modernist group f/64 to mind. A quick photo history lesson: f/64 was a group formed by photographer Alfred Stieglitz, as a counter to the Pictorialist movement, which I will discuss with the category of Impressionism. A succinct mission statement given by member Edward Weston reads, "The camera should be used for a recording of life, for rendering the very substance and quintessence of the thing itself, whether it be polished steel or palpitating flesh." The reason the group was called f/64 was because they often chose to photograph using that f/stop, which is the lowest, and which gives the most sharpness to an image. If you choose to take the approach of Realism (or Modernism) when shooting landscape, you may want to try shooting at this f/stop.

Impressionism is the opposing force to Pictorialism, as most Modernists would agree. This style of landscape is more about the atmosphere or drama in a picture; it's about emotion and intent. Where Modernism/Realism is about capturing a documentary picture that is true to life, Pictorialism/Impressionism is a more craft-based, fine art enterprise. Even today, I would venture to say that the majority of popular landscape images are Impressionistic. The reason these kinds of pictures are so loved is because they rely on atmosphere as well as craft.

Atmosphere is all around us, and while we may not notice it in daily life, it has a huge impact on our perception of a photograph. Atmosphere is both literally the weight and presence of the air in a photograph and the impression it leaves on us. The weight I refer to denotes our spatial ability to sense depth, or the presence of foreground, middle ground, and background. Differing atmospheres, such as a sunny clear day versus a day with heavy cloud cover affect our ability to see these different spatial areas. With these differences in vision, we are also affected psychologically. This, in conjunction with color, affects how we feel about a photograph.

Atmosphere in landscape always has a color or feel to it, which can make all the difference to our perception. If, for example, an image is made up of rich reds and golds, it can convey a sense of glory or power. If it leans more toward the red than the gold, it may feel more menacing. A calm, contemplative photo, by contrast, may be made up of cool greens and blues. And an image that is moody, with a high contrast of black and white, or that is heavy, with dark purples and blues, can convey a troubled atmosphere.

Atmospheric perception can also be affected by use of selective focus, depth of field, and composition, all of which I will discuss both in technical and aesthetic terms in Chapter 5. For example, if you have an image with a heavy, foggy atmosphere, and you choose to shoot it at a shallow depth of field, you could either create an airy, dreamlike feel, or an oppressive horror movie mood, depending on your choice of color. I will also discuss this further in a later chapter.

The second attribute of Impressionism/Pictorialsm that differentiates it from Realism/Modernism is the craft. By craft, I mean the level of care and choice of technique that goes into the final print of the photo. That is not to say that realistic, documentary photos aren't well done. All it means is that they're very straightforward, while Pictorialism allows for more freedom of expression in the printing. This includes things like dodging and burning for artistic effect, using a special paper, or using an alternative process printing technique.

The third kind of landscape work, as briefly discussed above, is Abstract. Abstraction requires the visible landscape to be reduced to interpretive shapes and colors. The emotional impact of the image is considered far more important than the actual, physical content of the image. How Stieglitz would have shuddered!

These types of pictures can be intentionally shallow or blurred, a simple mechanism, or can move further toward the feeling of painting by having the sky, sea, or grass fill the entire frame. While these images can have a horizon line, they aren't required to. Those without such can be somewhat disconcerting and, in my mind, quite interesting.

Now that you know a little bit about the history of landscape photography and all its varieties, let's get started on making photographs!

Chapter 2
Understanding Your Camera Settings

This is the most technical chapter of this book. I have tried to make it as simple and non-intimidating as possible.

Learning to control your camera may be difficult to grasp at first, but with practice and an underlying understanding of how your camera works, it'll be easier to make good photographs. Not only that, but you will also find that your ability to consistently take well-exposed photos improves.

If you shoot digitally, you may be wondering why this is important. If a photo isn't properly exposed, you can just delete it and try again, right? Better yet, you can fix it in Photoshop! While both of these statements are technically true, these aren't good habits to develop. Think of it like this: if you spend all your time deleting photos and messing aimlessly with settings to try and get the look you want, you'll only get frustrated. You run the risk of losing good light, especially during the *golden hour* (we'll discuss this term in the next chapter) and you may even give up. If you know exactly how to get what you want, however, you'll spend more time taking good photographs. This, in turn, leads to more desirable images without as much thought.

If you still think that you'll just fix your photos later, you could be startled to find that it may not even be possible. Beginning photographers often think of Photoshop as a magic catchall of mistakes. Sometimes, though, photos are just too technically incorrect to be saved. You could spend hours laboring over one problem that could have been corrected at the initial taking in a few seconds. Additionally, after you spend all these hours correcting, you may find that the photo now looks too fake to be useable. The easiest way to make a good landscape is to take a good image from the start, which can then be enhanced, rather than saved, by Photoshop.

Firstly, you should make sure to always shoot in RAW format. If you don't shoot with Canon, you may have the choice to shoot in DNG, which is also a RAW file format. RAW files record the most information, allowing you to make the most effective edits and get the most out of your pictures. In addition, I want to mention that, when you are finished editing, you can save your images as jpegs, which are small and good for things like previews and web use. However, you should never *just* save as jpegs. Should you need to do further editing or large prints, you'll want to have the RAW files available to you because of their superior quality. At the very least, convert your RAW files to DNG or the similar TIF format, both of which are smaller but still contain a larger amount of information.

The second thing I want to discuss is the automatic settings on your camera. Most cameras these days do a good job getting an okay exposure, but the problem with exposure that's just "okay" is seldom what you really want. If you aren't already familiar with how cameras work, I would recommend using your automatic settings as a starting point, and then metering for your focal point. Another method is to meter for a middle grey, and then adjust your exposure to something more appropriate for your subject.

As you learn to control your camera, it would serve you to memorize the common f/stops and shutter speeds. Digital cameras often include half steps, which can become confusing when trying to figure out the correct exposure. In addition, learn as much as you can about equivalent exposures. These are different combinations of aperture and shutter speed that will provide the same exposure (or amount of light coming into the lens), but with different depths of field and amount (or lack thereof) of motion blur.

Once you've experimented with your camera and established a basis of equivalent exposures, you'll be able to use the AV and TV buttons on your camera. These stand for aperture and shutter priority, respectively, and allow you to set the value for whichever you've selected. The camera then meters the other value to give you an appropriate exposure. Using the AV and TV buttons can be a good midpoint in becoming able to use manual settings properly.

One good way to achieve an image with lots of selective movement involves a tripod and some math. Set your camera up and select a very slow shutter speed, such as f/30, coupled with a corresponding f/stop for good exposure. (Often, your camera's meter will over-compensate for you, and you'll want to *stop down,* or close one to two stops—making the f/stop number bigger—to avoid overexposure). The good thing about digital photography is that you can put your camera on manual to experiment with this technique and see the results right away. You can also immediately see the results of bracketing, which is a technique involving various exposures of the same image. This can be a good practice run if you're planning to shoot in low light on film. You'll just want to make sure that the ISO (ASA) of your digital camera is set to the same ISO as the film you'll be using.

If you want an even longer exposure than your camera allows, there's a button for that. Well, two actually. The bulb setting (B) is used by pressing and holding until the desired exposure time has elapsed, and then it is released. The time (T) setting is used similarly, except that it is pressed once to open, and then the shutter stays open until it's pressed again. This can be especially handy for situations where you don't want to stand and hold a button, such as for exposures that last thirty minutes or more.

To make a quick exposure that freeze motion in action, you'll need a fast shutter speed. As with any other type of exposure, although there are guidelines, you'll have to play around with your camera to find the best settings for your needs. In addition, the faster the motion, the faster your shutter speed will need to be in order to "freeze" it.

I want to caution you on the use of very high ISOs. In analog photography, the ISO is what tells the camera how sensitive the film is. Basically, the faster the film speed, the more sensitive it is to light. The ISO setting on a digital camera operates on the same principle. You're telling the camera to adapt to a different sensitivity. On newer digital cameras, ISOs can exceed 3200 and still produce a very good quality photograph. However, if you have an older camera or are shooting with film, higher ISOs can result in pictures that cross the line between grainy and noisy. While obvious grain can be a conscious aesthetic choice, noise never is. Don't default to cranking up your ISO just because it's easier than figuring out the proper combination of aperture and shutter speed.

Chapter 3
Finding Beautiful Light and Why You Should Shoot in All Types of Weather

I'll tell you a secret: the only thing you truly need to know to make a good landscape is *how to find beautiful light*. If you have beautiful light and a good atmosphere, the photo will be gorgeous. You simply have to be looking around you—*seeing*—at all times.

You can work in many different qualities of light, and none of them are wrong. Some people may disagree, citing that light at noon is terrible for photographs, for example, but we'll address that later.

If you are just starting to shoot landscape, my first suggestion would be to make use of the *golden hour*. The golden hour actually happens twice a day, in the morning after sunrise and in the evening just before dusk. (There's a reason so many people like sunrise and sunset photos!) The golden hour is also much more interesting when viewed over a landscape. The light is absolutely radiant, and because the sun isn't directly overhead, it doesn't cast harsh shadows. Gentle shadows are incredibly pleasing because they soften the atmosphere, and the light appears much more even than at other times of day. Everything glows and can be seen with great detail and clarity.

While both sunrise and sunset produce a similar effect, they are different from one another. This difference may be barely perceptible, but nonetheless, it's present. At sunrise, the light is more neat and pale, with lighter colors such as yellows, reds, and pinks. Reds also tend to be stronger at sunrise. At sunset, conversely, light fades faster, and results in vibrant purples and rich oranges. The difference is slight, but if you go out and shoot at both times of day, you will soon discover which time you prefer.

Another type of light that's really great for any photographer is that of an overcast day. Many people don't believe this because because an overcast day lacks the beautiful cloud formations that are so common and loved in landscape photos. But as with the golden hour, the light is great for photography. This is because the sun's rays get dispersed through the clouds, casting even light on everything. Your picture will be free of harsh shadows.

If you want a picture with this smooth light *and* impressive clouds, there are two methods to achieve this. The first is to shoot the landscape itself in the overcast light, then come back another day to photograph the clouds. This, of course, will require compositing the two pictures together. Or, if the day has a perfect sky, but would otherwise be too bright, you can use a neutral density filter to lower the amount of light coming into your lens. This will not affect your shadows, but it will help control brightness. Other filters, such as red which has a lower contrast, can be used to achieve different effects, which will be discussed later.

Your time for landscape photography isn't limited to sunrise/set and overcast days, however. Shooting midmorning is still generally permissible by most photographers, but you have to be careful if you're going for a look that requires smooth light. As the day approaches noon, shadows will grow harsher. This is because, as the sun gets higher, shadows get shorter and darker. The light is coming from directly above, and with nothing to diffuse it from the sides, shadows can look black and unflattering. The afternoon progresses, the light gets better and better again, similar to how it was in midmorning. It's still not as good as the golden hour, but it's better. The reason the golden hour is so pleasing is because the shadows are long, and therefore, cover more of the landscape, diffusing the light.

The exception to this rule, again, is an overcast day, which will provide you with even light as long as the cloud cover remains.

Despite the fact that shadows are harsh and can be unflattering at noon, it's still a valid time of day to shoot if you know how to make it work to your advantage. If you happen to like the shadows, use them. Many people may tell you that it's technically wrong, but that doesn't mean you can't create a great, dramatic photo. Do some playing around and make the shadows work for you. You can do this, for example, by shooting from a direction that causes them to make interesting patterns on your subject, thereby using the light to create an abstract landscape.

On the other hand, if you need to shoot at noon because you have no other options, take advantage of the shade to control your light. You can use natural shade, or create your own. Often, the falling light through dappled shade can provide interesting, lovely patterns, especially if you're interested in light studies and abstractions. To create more even shade that will be reminiscent of an overcast day, you can use an umbrella, mounted over the camera, to diffuse the light.

If you're not so minimalistic with your shots, you can also opt to bring lights as well as umbrellas, as long as you have a source of electricity. By placing a light to the side of your subject, just as in portraiture photography, you are creating a fill for your subject. This technique, however, can usually only be employed on a small scale, because most of us don't have the resources to light a huge scene. (To do so, you'd need the budget and equipment of a film set, or of Gregory Crewdson's photos.) This means that the subjects you *could* light with this technique would have to be relatively small. This would work well, then, for photographing things like flowers or other plant details.

Night shooting is altogether a different beast. Your biggest enemy when it comes to getting a good landscape at night is a shaking camera. With any sort of landscape, unless you're shooting on a high f/stop with a correspondingly quick shutter speed (as correlates to a correct exposure, of course), you'll want to use a tripod. On a sunny day, you can probably get away with f/8 and a 60th of a second exposure without being *too* overexposed, but I wouldn't recommend shooting any more open or slower than that without a tripod. So of course, at night, a tripod is essential. Otherwise you'll end up with images that are barely decipherable, badly affected by the combination of low light and camera shake. As you know from the previous chapter, you can control the exposure of a night image using either the night setting on your camera (which can be a good starting point, but I wouldn't recommend stopping there), or by using a manual combination of appropriate ISO, shutter speed and aperture.

Aside from using a larger aperture and/or slow shutter speed, another good technique is to use the light that is available to you. Use the glow of street lamps or windows to your advantage. Shooting detail is also a good approach. Often, detail areas, such as the sides of buildings, will be illuminated more than the entire façade. And when you zoom in, you're letting in more light , which, in this case, is good.

As in the previous chapter, I want to caution against the impulse to just up your ISO when shooting at night. While this is a quick fix, the grain can quickly cease being grain and become noise, which is distracting and hard to remove, especially in color.

Now you know the optimal way to shoot in any lighting condition. If you are new to the genre of landscape, or if you just need a refresher, I would not suggest starting with night photography. Instead, learn to control your camera in the kind light of the golden hour, then progress to complicated techniques as your skills increase.

Other than just light types, you should also consider shooting in all weather. Depending on the type of weather involved, you may need to take some precautions, especially with regards to personal safety. However, if you just want to try shooting in the rain, go for it!

There are all kinds of waterproof camera covers sold by reputable dealers of photography accessories. If you don't have the money to invest in something like that at the moment, a clear plastic bag will work in a pinch. In this case, I wouldn't recommend staying outside too long. I do suggest, though, always carrying a protective covering of some sort in any conditions, in case it starts to rain or snow.

Now that most of the technical stuff has been discussed, the majority of the remaining chapters will focus on why we make the pictures we do and how to make the pictures we want.

Chapter 4
The Importance of
Composition and Other
Design Elements

As with any other art or design concept, you must consider the elements and principles of design when composing your landscape images. These are all things you may already know, but a refresher can't hurt.

The *elements of design* are: *line, shape, direction, color, size, texture,* and *value.* The *principles of design* are: *balance, gradation, repetition, harmony, contrast, dominance,* and *unity.* All of these aspects come together to form what is referred to as a composition. Composition is not only what the subject of your landscape is, such as a tree in a field, but also how it is arranged. Is the tree out in the field by itself, or is it surrounded by a repetition of other plant life? Is it smack in the middle of the frame, or is it off to one side? Does it appear to be above or below the perceived horizon line? All of these considerations will alter how a viewer interprets your photo. When you're about to take a photo, ask yourself which of these design principles is attracting you.

One of the best principles to think about with any composition is *line.* Use the natural lines and shapes of a scene to guide the eye of the viewer through the picture. Try not to let lines in the image lead off of the picture plane, unless it serves to carry the eye sequentially through the series as a whole. It's much more interesting to use line to move *through* the image, perhaps leading to the focal point or main subject.

When I talk about a line in this context, it can be anything that's within the scene. Vines, branches, rivers, and the curl of foam on a wave are just a few examples. Closely related to line is shape, which is also something to watch out for. If the branches of a tree curve to create a heart, that might be something interesting to look at. Shapes also occur in vast repetition in nature, such as the shapes of leaves. Look for interesting breaks in patterns, or perhaps at the pattern as an engaging image in its own right.

When I talk about *harmony*, what I mean is how the image flows and works together. This incorporates everything from the list of elements and principles above. Consider whether your color palette is similar or dissimilar, whether the arrangement of your image is weighted or perfectly balanced. All of this contributes to harmony.

Before you can break any compositional rules, you have to follow them so that you know *how, why,* and *when* to break them. The easiest way to check the overall balance of your image is to use the *rule of thirds*. When shooting an image, most beginners may feel the need to put the subject right in the middle of the frame. However, most of the time this severe evenness is *too* balanced, and in order for the eye to move naturally around the image, the subject can't be dead center. (There are, of course, exceptions to this rule. Say you have a tree with some interesting, arching, gnarled branches. Placing the trunk in the middle and allowing the branches to flow off erratically can make the picture just off-center enough for it to work.)

To see if your image is following the rule, take your image and divide it into thirds horizontally, and then again vertically. It's really easy to do in Photoshop . . . just go to View>New Guide, and place the lines at equal intervals. If your image follows the rule, you will find that focal points (the more interesting, dynamic parts of the image) will fall along an intersections of the lines.

To play around with the rule, try moving your focal point to one extreme side, or to the top or bottom. Alternatively, you can leave the focal point where it is, and then shift the camera up or down, which changes the position of the horizon line. Just as a horizon line changes in real life as we move or jump or go up a hill, you can create interest or even depth by moving the horizon line up or down. This technique is useful to eliminate the boring parts of a landscape . . . Who says that a landscape has to have a sky? Why does the land have to be the main part of the photo if what's really striking is the sky? Play around in different situations to figure out what works best.

I know I've spoken about color and light before, and I will do so again in the editing portions of this book, but I feel it's important to note that the power of both should not be underestimated. Both color and light serve functions other than what they are; color and light can provide balance, direction, unity, and line for the eye to follow. Color and light are power and will often make the first, most immediate impression on your audience. Saturated color denotes a different mood than desaturated, and darker colors make us feel differently than light ones.

There are also various useful color schemes (think rules about color rather than specific colors) that can be utilized to sway the emotions of a viewer. And before you think that you can't control the color of a landscape—yes, you can. All it takes is knowing what you're looking for, and then choosing how to manipulate it.

Here are the four main types of color schemes: monochromatic, complementary, analogous, and split complementary.

Contrary to popular belief, monochromatic does not mean black and white, although a monochromatic color scheme could be the variances of grey that fall between black and white. It simply means one color. If you were to take a textural picture of some foliage for example, that would be a monochromatic image. The image is all green but different shades of green.

Next is analogous, and all this means is that the colors lie next to each other on the color wheel. A color palette comprised of greens and blues and blue-greens could be categorized as analogous. A seascape would be such a photograph. A picture of purple, fuchsia, and red flowers is also analogous.

Complementary might be the easiest color scheme to find unadulterated in nature. Complementary simply refers to colors that oppose each other on the color wheel. Poinsettias and red roses come with a natural complementary color palette.

The last and most complicated scheme is split complementary. It works under the same principle as a complementary scheme. You pick a color, say for example, green. Going across the color wheel, its complement is red. Instead of just using red, however, you would also use the adjacent colors, which are orange and purple. All four of these colors and their variations would be permissible in keeping with the scheme.

Now that you know how to spot these schemes, you can make more informed decisions about the prominent colors in your landscapes.

Light is also a useful tool, in that it can transform the mood of something that may have the colors of an opposing mood. If you were to go to a carnival, for instance, where all the colors are cheery, you could choose to photograph it at a time of day that would provide deep shadow, thereby creating a more sinister feel.

The elements and principles of design, as listed above, are your tools. Without them, you have a snapshot instead of a piece of art.

Chapter 5
Don't Be Afraid!—Tools and Terms for a Beautiful Photograph

Now that you know these techniques for making an awesome landscape photograph, you'll probably want to go out and shoot! After all, you've got a camera and tripod. And while this is all well and good, there are a few more things you'll need before you begin.

When I go out to shoot, I always carry a small array of tools with me, both actual and photographic.

Regarding photographic tools, in addition to a tripod, you might also consider carrying things like clamps, a reflector, black and white flags, a light meter, filters, and an umbrella. You already know that the umbrella is for diffusing light, but reflectors and flags can come in handy for bouncing light toward or away from a subject. These aren't as important, though, as clamps, a meter, and filters. Clamps are just good to have in case it gets windy or you need to hold something that is moving and/or heavy. A light meter is good to have for double-checking your surroundings and making sure your camera is metering properly.

If you can't afford a good light meter (which is understandable—they're expensive!) you have two options. Either look up and print out an equivalent exposure sheet, or download an app for your smart phone. I find, however, that most apps are quite inaccurate. The one I *would* recommend is called Pinhole Assist, which costs about two dollars, as it's accurate enough and doesn't cost the hundreds or even thousands of dollars a proper light meter would be.

The next tool you should carry is a set of filters. It's very important to have at least a basic pack of these around to take on shoots. Packs of filters (or gels) vary, but will typically include the colors red, green, yellow, and blue. A neutral density filter is also good to have. And while you can buy them to fit your lens, I find it's just as easy to have someone hold one in front of the lens.

Filters fix a variety of technical issues so you won't have to correct for them in Photoshop (although, admittedly, a filter layer in Photoshop will solve some problems too.) Red gels help to fix low contrast and will also darken the image. This can help to bring in those pesky cloudy skies. Yellow darkens your image, green lightens other green things (useful if your foliage is in shadow and starts to block up), and blue lightens skies and lowers contrast. Filters work via complementary colors, as we discussed in the previous chapter. A filter lightens whatever color it is, and darkens the complement. This is the easiest way to remember what each does. That's why red filters are so good for landscape: they amplify the greens. To see this effect for yourself, try it out in Photoshop. Color filters work best on black and white images.

Neutral density filters reduce the amount of light coming into the lens and are generally greyish. They can reduce the glare of an over-bright background, and can also be used to motion blur an image while still maintaining a proper exposure. If you never keep any other filters in your bag, keep a red and a neutral density one.

Aside from your photographic tools, I would also recommend keeping a small toolkit and first aid kit handy.

In addition to knowing how to control the exposure and how to compose a good photo, you should be familiar with a few other photography terms: *depth of field* and *focal point*.

Depth of field refers to how far away the eye can see, and in a photograph, that's important. Often, a photo is referred to as either having a shallow or deep depth of field. For most landscape photographs, you'll want to employ a deep depth of field, which allows your viewer to see far off into the distance. Of course, depth of field can be affected by things such as haze, cloud cover, and rain, but these factors can actually produce more depth depending on where they fall. Deep depth of field is achieved by using a higher (or smaller fraction) f/stop, such as f/16, f/32, or higher. Shallow depth of field is achieved by using a lower (or larger fraction) f/stop, such as f/8, f/4, or lower. Shallow depth of field can be useful for bringing an important foreground object into focus, and letting the background fall away.

Focal point is just a fancy term for your subject, or whatever it is you're focusing your photograph on. However far away your subject is will determine the focal length of your lens for that picture. In other words, it's how far zoomed in or out you are from your subject. Be aware that different lenses have different focal lengths, so make sure that you are adequately close or far away from your subject to achieve the effect you want. Your focal length will also determine the scale of your subject in relation to its surroundings. In general, the further away your focal point, the smaller your subject looks. You can use this knowledge to manipulate your photo by making things in the frame appear smaller or larger than they actually are.

Chapter 6
Expressing Yourself Through Landscapes

In order to truly create an expressive print, you need to have taken a photograph that is technically proficient. Many people think that once they have a beautiful, well-exposed photograph with a strong composition, they're done. While you can choose to stop there, it's not necessary. There are a world of possibilities beyond just taking a technically competent photograph, though, as I've stated, it's an essential starting point.

For starters, don't worry if the way you begin to photograph is by walking around and shooting things that interest you. Lots of great portfolios begin this way. After you've shot a fair amount of images, you should sit down and look at them as a whole. This will help you to identify elements that the pictures have in common. Should you choose to create a series, rather than just a single image, the qualities that you identify will help you to consciously unify the body of work as you shoot more.

Take into consideration all of the components we've discussed. What is similar in composition, in color, in line, in movement, in mood or in atmosphere? Most of this selection and grouping takes place without much conscious thought—we just automatically know which images flow together. There are underlying psychological elements that guide this decision-making process.

There are two ways, in the digital realm, to go about grouping images. Either you can do it with Lightroom, using ratings, flags and quick collections to rank and eliminate images. Or you can do it the old fashioned way, which is my preferred method. Print small proofs of your images and arrange them on a table or floor, moving them and grouping them by hand. Having used both methods on the same catalogue of images, I can tell you that it's possible for your choices to differ depending on which method you choose. It's not that one way is better than the other, but holding and moving the images by hand causes us to think differently than sorting them on a computer. Try both and see which you prefer. If you're shooting film, you can use your contact sheets as a reference, or scan them in and use one of the above methods to do your grouping.

As you're grouping, you should not only consider the principles and elements of design, but the conceptual reasons behind what you're shooting. Other than just being beautiful or dramatic, what do your landscapes *say?* Portfolios with a reason behind them are a lot more unified than ones that are solely aesthetically pleasing. Luckily, in the past years, environment has become a huge political issue, which makes landscape photography a viable subject with many standpoints to choose from. Think about *why* you chose to photograph the places you did. Was it a personal connection? Is this a place that has been reclaimed by nature? Or is it trashed, lacking conventional beauty and making a statement about how we care (or don't care) for the Earth?

You may be thinking that you didn't have a concept in mind to begin with, that you just shot what seemed interesting to you. If this is the case, that's fine, but it doesn't change the fact that you can still come up with a reason these particular photos are important to you. Therein lies your concept.

Now I want to talk about determining your overall print aesthetic. When I say print aesthetic, I mean how you want your finished image to look, whether or not you intend to print it out. If you do intend to print, there will be some extra considerations to keep in mind.

If you use Lightroom to edit, feel free to use their top-down workflow, which is pretty efficient for all your basic edits. If you use Photoshop, I would still recommend a similar approach regarding the basics. Match your white balances and refine exposures first, then adjust your lighting. Unless you shot all of your landscapes in the same light on the same day, the adjustments won't be exactly the same. Though you should consider the light when first shooting, I want to point out that subtle lighting changes can affect the mood of your photo drastically.

Next, consider the contrast. Do you want your landscapes to be light and airy, ethereal? Or are they meant to be moody, taut, anticipatory? If you shot a beautiful sunny scene of a pasture and horses, you may choose the former, while if there were storm clouds on that same horizon, you may be inclined to choose the latter. Though many factors contribute to the overall mood, contrast is one that can have a huge affect just by itself.

This means that, with contrast, you usually need less than you think you do. New landscape photographers, wanting their images to look dramatic and exciting, will often bump the contrast up fifty or a hundred percent. Resist the urge. This much contrast will just make an image block up, and look less than dimensional. (*Blocking up* means that all of the blacks in the image consolidate together, making the image look blocky and flat). This can be a look if it's done intentionally from the start, but since the point of landscape is to capture beauty and detail, I really wouldn't recommend it.

The same is true of saturation that is too high. Instead, I would suggest using a combination of the vibrance sliders and the color balance ones. In this way, you can isolate and control only the colors you want to affect, rather than the whole image. Say for example that you want the reds and the oranges to pop a little bit more in the sky. If red and orange are only really present in the sky, go ahead and use the corresponding sliders to achieve your desired hues. Alternatively, if one section of a photo needs some pop, you can mask everything except that area and apply the color correction on top of that mask.

Another corrective tool that is simultaneously underrated and overused is called the clarity slider. For those of you who haven't used it, it does exactly what it says. It's basically a glorified sharpening and contrast tool. Now, you don't have as much control with the clarity slider as I would like, so use it sparingly. I don't really like it for portraiture, but for landscape, it can give that little bit of a hyper realistic pop without going to the trouble of HDR, which I will go over in the next chapter.

The techniques and tools for editing mentioned above are just a small sampling of the tools both Photoshop and Lightroom provide. Explore them, watch tutorials, take workshops, and increase your knowledge. Just as with camera settings, the more you know, the more control you have, and the finer and more nuanced your images become.

If you choose to make prints of your images, there are a few other considerations to bear in mind. Talking extensively about printing would warrant a whole other book, so I'll just give some basic pointers.

First, you'll need to think about what kind of paper you want to use, and there are thousands to choose from. From a basic point of view, there are *matte*, *luster*, and *glossy* finishes. Matte is beautiful, and some papers can look like velvet if properly printed, but they also have a tendency to block up darker hues, and your photograph may need to be lightened considerably before you're satisfied with the result. Luster papers (a similar finish is called *pearl*) are halfway between matte and gloss, so they provide enough gloss to prevent blocking in the darks without hitting you over the head with shiny, smooth texture. Finally, there's glossy, which is probably the most popularly selected in commercial printing. People like it because colors and texture really show, and of course, it shines.

Now that you know (or have been refreshed) in basic Photoshop editing techniques, let's talk about some more advanced techniques that you can choose to employ.

Chapter 7
Every Photographer Has a Panorama . . . And Other Thoughts

I once had a professor who said that every great photographer has a panorama. This seems to be true, as I've found very few exceptions. Panorama is something every good landscape photographer should learn. In fact, though I have seen panoramas used in other types of conceptual work, it is most popular within the genre of landscapes. This is with very obvious and good reason. If you're going to shoot a landscape, why not a full view of it?

Making a panorama is incredibly simple now with a Photoshop plugin, although you may find it impressive to note that the first panoramas were made entirely by hand in a darkroom. Most of us today don't have that kind of patience, although you can still choose to try it if you'd like.

Here's a quick overview of how to create a panorama in Photoshop. First, of course, you have to have your images. An easy way to explain how these images must be taken is included with the iPhone. When you go to create a panorama with your phone, the software instructs you to keep your phone level with a straight line displayed on the screen. When you craft your pictures using a DSLR, the concept is the same. In order for the panoramic stitching software to work properly, the pictures you use need to follow the same horizon line as much as possible. Therefore, I would not suggest attempting to hand-hold your camera. Put it in your starting spot and shoot several images, and then rotate your tripod a bit. You want to make sure that some of the information in the first image is also included in the second. This way, the program will know that's where the image is meant to merge. It's important to take several of the same image so you can choose the perfect fit. More than that, the more images you use to create a panorama, the more detailed it will be. Keep doing this until you've gone in a full circle. This may go without saying, but make sure that all of your images are taken in the same format (horizontal or vertical).

Next, you're going to import your images into Photoshop and open the dialog box for panorama. The commands are File>Automate>Photomerge. After you select your images and hit OK, you'll have the option to try different types of panorama to see what looks best. If none of them do, that's when you know you need to follow your horizon line with more accuracy. Also, keep in mind that if you are using a lot of very large files to compose your panorama, it may take a long time to stitch together. I've also had the program crash, so make sure your computer has enough processing power to handle this feature.

Another popular technique, both recently and in the genre of landscape, is HDR. HDR stands for *high dynamic range* imaging, and essentially extracts a larger range of information, rendering the photo to look more true to life. If overdone, HDR can easily look hyper real or even fake. I would suggest then, to only use HDR when it is for the overall benefit of the image. HDR is especially good for those pesky images that just won't expose correctly. An example: say you have a scene where the background is a bright sunny day, and the mid-to-foreground is in shade. What you can then do is take a picture for each, and merge the two in HDR to make the whole photo correctly exposed.

Another method to HDR is to take several differing exposures of the same scene and merge them. It's much the same concept as the panorama—the more exposures you make, the more detailed the result. Basically, what you're doing is bracketing. Make an image with the proper exposure for the scene (or part of the scene, if you have something like the situation mentioned above), then bracket half a stop below, a stop below, a stop and a half below, etc. Do the same in the opposite direction.

To merge the images, again go to File>Automate>Merge to HDR Pro. You will then be taken to a dialog box that will allow you to adjust your shadows, highlights, and saturation, as with non-HDR photos. You can also control other, more specific factors such as edge glow and gamma. There are also a variety of presets you can scroll through, to get the image generally how you want it.

These are two specific ways to control the quality and style of your landscape. My favorite method, which, I feel, achieves the most natural-looking landscape that still has a pop, is by doing the majority of your editing in Camera RAW. Camera RAW is a godsend, and can pull a lot of information out of a photo, because it is specifically meant for those RAW files. You may find, as I often do, that a simple edit in camera RAW brings enough out of an image to make it an absolute beauty. If not, by using Smart Objects in conjunction with Camera RAW, you can easily edit the same picture twice, once for shadow, and once for highlights, and then apply a layer mask to make the overall exposure appropriate. This technique will give you a still dynamic, yet more realistic looking image than HDR.

There is no wrong way to choose to process your images. Though do consider panorama, working in HDR, and working in Camera RAW if you really want your images to stand out.

Chapter 8
Don't Give Up (And Don't Make Excuses)

In doing my research for this book, I read a lot of reviews on other publications. One of the reviews that truly bothered me was one in which a reader said that a book was useless because the person simply did not have time to photograph during any of the suggested times of day.

As discussed in Chapter 3, there are certain light conditions that are considered optimal for shooting a landscape. These are the golden hours of the day, around daybreak and right before sunset, when, as the name suggests, the day turns a golden color. Now, as mentioned before, no one is saying that you *must* shoot during these times of day, or that if you choose not to, your landscape isn't going to be good. But if your reason for never shooting at these times of day is because you "don't have time," you may need to do some deeper thinking.

Do you not have time because you are legitimately too busy, or because you don't care? When something is important to you (as photography obviously is, or you wouldn't be reading this) you must make time to make it the best it can be.

In respect to the golden hour, use this lovely time to your advantage. You'll develop a sense, as the seasons change, of the approximate times it occurs. If you don't, you can always look up the times the day before, in preparation. If you can't shoot at the evening golden hour due to work or other responsibilities, plan to shoot at dawn. It's understandable not to want to get up before sunrise each day of the week, but choosing to do it one day a week is a good start. Even if it's the only day of the week you get to capture that quality of light, you're still giving yourself the opportunity to do so. And just as with any other habit or routine, you may find that as time passes, you will wake early enough to shoot on a daily basis.

If, however, you hold a job where you are at work at this time, perhaps focus your energy on shooting during the golden hour before dusk. Shoot before you go to work if you have a night shift, or arrange to have breaks around that time. Maybe postpone going home from work five or ten minutes to shoot in the golden light. It's all about finding small niches of time in which to shoot, rather than making every shoot into a planned production. You never know what you'll see when you're out doing the most mundane of daily tasks.

The easiest way to get into the habit of seeing, and of shooting regularly, is to carry a camera with you everywhere. This does not mean you have to carry a large DSLR everywhere; it could be a pocket-sized point and shoot, a disposable film camera, or even your phone. In fact, given that everyone owns a smartphone now (or at least a phone capable of taking pictures) the excuse, "I don't have a camera" is now obsolete.

You may think that you need a large, snazzy camera to take good images, but that isn't true. Some of the most interesting images come from Polaroids, Instagram, and pinhole cameras. You may be surprised by what you can come up with using a non-DSLR camera. And even if the resulting image isn't exactly what you're looking for, it is better to have a record of the place and time than to be without it. This way, you can go back to the place at a different time (or the same, if you want a similar look and better quality) and reshoot. These kinds of "test shots" are actually really good to do—they can help you see composition or lighting you didn't notice the first time.

I really enjoy Instagram as a tool, because when you post an image, you have the option to log it on your map. This can be very helpful, especially if you've been out exploring, so that you can use your phone to relocate it later. If you choose to go the analog route, carry a small notebook with you so that you can record what you shot, where it was, the time of day, and your settings. Even with Instagram, this may prove to be a useful practice, but it really depends on personal preference and how technical you are when shooting landscapes.

I strongly believe that you should attempt to shoot every day, especially when you're just starting out. However, a lot of photographers mistake this for meaning that you should shoot *a lot* each day. This is not true, and in fact, I think you should limit yourself to a small amount each day. (If you shoot analog, you understand that this is partly to conserve materials). Whether digital or analog, however, shooting fewer pictures means you are focusing more on quality, as opposed to quantity. If you're having to spend time thinking about your light and your composition rather than just snapping away, you'll soon develop an inherent knowledge of what looks good and what doesn't. The proportion of good photographs as opposed to just usable ones will go up as well.

Landscape photography is a difficult craft. No matter what, don't give up. Just because it looks easy doesn't mean it is. Be patient with yourself and give yourself time to learn. Use the techniques described above to get into the habit of seeing. Experiment with analog and digital, low contrast and high contrast, black and white versus color. If you don't get a shot the first time, try it again and again. Many of the best photographs that appear to be spontaneous actually took multiple tries, or even compositing multiple photos, to achieve the desired look.

Conclusion

Having come to the end of this book, you should be well on your way to becoming a competent, if not prolific, landscape photographer. I feel that the most important part of this book had to do with helping you understand how to see, and why you see the way you do. Technique can be taught, and is ever evolving. It requires constant self-education to keep up. But an eye for content, meaning, and composition cannot be taught in any other way than constant experience.

To become a great landscape photographer, you must first have a passion for the land, and the drive to look around you constantly. Find what interests you and photograph it. Constantly question why you're interested in the landscapes you make. What is the reason behind them? What drives you to make them, and process them the way you do? This is the meat, the lifeblood of your portfolio: it's all about you.

Now, knowing how to control your camera will give you the time to focus more on why and what you make, rather than how. Knowing what times of day produce what kinds of light gives you the ability to choose when you want to shoot for achieving your best pictures.

With practice, you'll become more aware, even subconsciously, of what scene you're composing when you look through the lens, as well as what works and why it works.

If you run into a jam, you now know some ways to solve the problem, as well as which essential tools to always take with you on a shoot.

Processing your images should now be a cinch. Make Photoshop work for you.

Above all, keep looking, keep seeing, and keep shooting beautiful landscapes.

Did you Like "Landscape Photography"?

Before you go, I'd like to say thank you so much for purchasing my book.

I know you could have picked from dozens of books on this subject, but you took a chance with mine, and I'm truly grateful for that.

So, once again, a big thanks for downloading this book and reading all the way to the end—I truly appreciate it.

Now I'd like to ask for a small favor if you don't mind:

Would you be so kind as to take a minute of your time and leave a review for this book on Amazon?

This feedback will help me continue to write the kind of books that help you get results. And if you loved it, then please feel free to let me know! :)